Dinosaurs and Their Young

Russell Freedman

illustrated by Leslie Morrill

Holiday House/New York

Text copyright © 1983 by Russell Freedman
Illustrations copyright © 1983 by Leslie Morrill
All rights reserved
Printed in the United States of America

Library of Congress Cataloging in Publication Data

Freedman, Russell.
Dinosaurs and their young.

Summary: Explains the recent discovery of the fossilized remains of duckbill dinosaur eggs and the young which hatched from them and conjectures that some dinosaurs may have cared for their young.
1. Dinosaurs—Juvenile literature.   [1. Dinosaurs]
I. Morrill, Leslie, ill.   II. Title.
QE862.D5F73   1983·   567.9'1   83-6160
ISBN 0-8234-0496-X

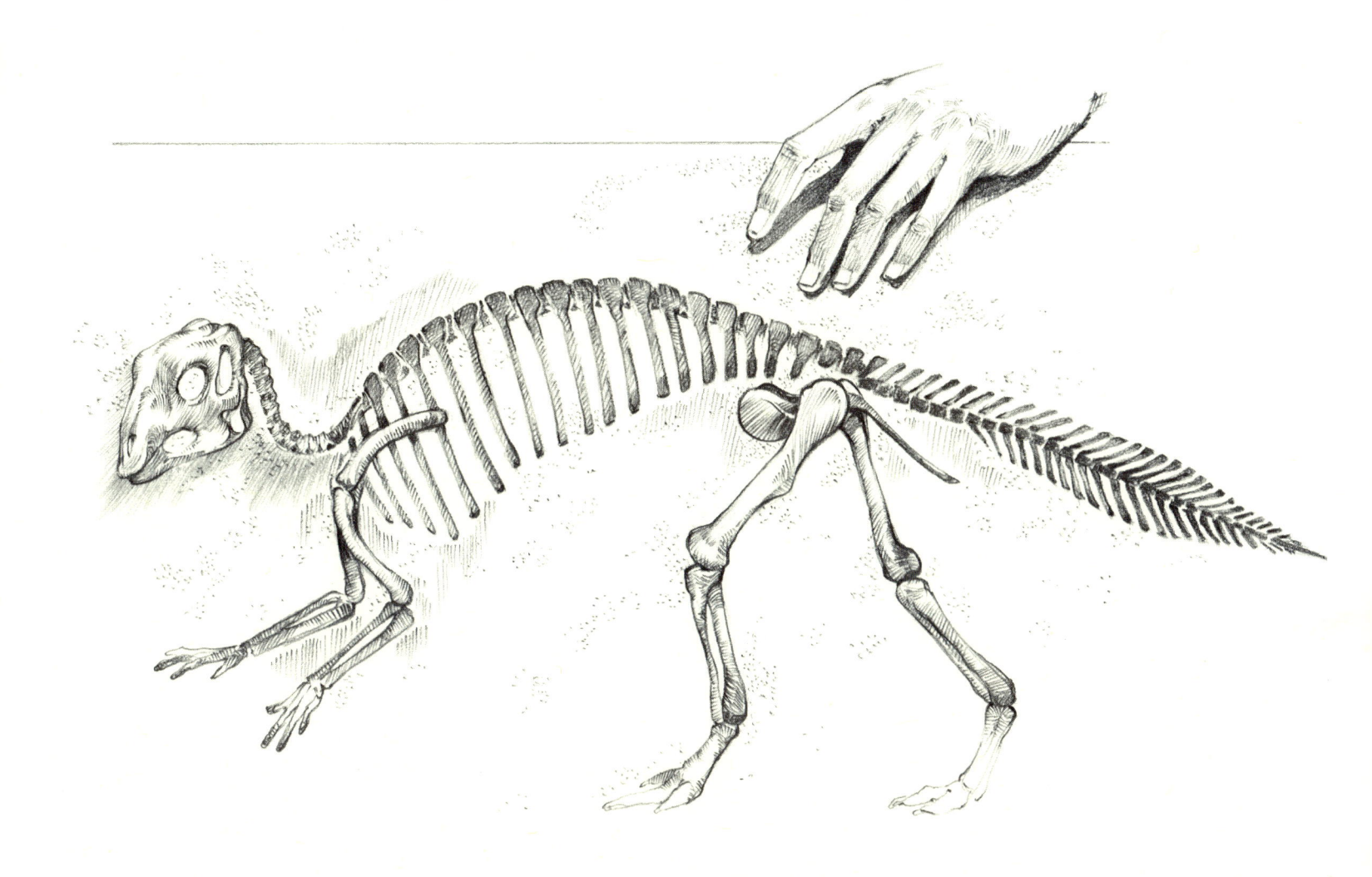

This is the skeleton of a baby dinosaur. Its bones were found in Montana in 1978.

The bones of other baby dinosaurs were found nearby. They caused great excitement when they were discovered, because they changed our thinking about dinosaurs and their young.

Scientists tell us that the last dinosaurs died about 60 million years ago. They left behind fossils—bones, eggs and footprints that have mostly turned to stone. By finding fossils and studying them, scientists try to learn what dinosaurs looked like and how they lived.

5

common Garter Snake

land Iguana (ig-WAH-na)

Most scientists believe that dinosaurs were reptiles. They belonged to the same group of animals as lizards, snakes, turtles and crocodiles. Like today's reptiles, dinosaurs had scaly skin and laid hard-shelled eggs.

Eastern Box Turtle

But they were different from modern reptiles in many ways. Some dinosaurs were much bigger than any reptiles living today. Some were faster and smarter. Some may have been more like warm-blooded birds than like cold-blooded reptiles.

Modern reptiles bury their eggs or hide them. But they do not usually guard the eggs. When baby lizards, snakes and turtles hatch, they are on their own. They never see their parents.

Crocodiles are different. They're the only reptiles living today that watch over their newly hatched young. A mother crocodile guards her babies for weeks or months. Of all the reptiles, crocodiles are the closest relatives of the dinosaurs.

Did dinosaurs leave their eggs, like lizards, snakes and turtles? Or did they guard their eggs and young, as crocodiles do?

Unhatched dinosaur eggs have been found in many parts of the world. In 1922, large numbers of eggs were discovered in the Gobi desert of Mongolia. They were the first eggs ever found that clearly belonged to dinosaurs.

The eggs had been buried in sand about 100 million years ago. They had been laid in neat circles. Each egg was about 8 inches long—longer than your hand. Some of the eggs still held the bones of unhatched babies.

Protoceratops young

The eggs belonged to a dinosaur called *Protoceratops* (pro-toh-SER-uh-tops). Scientists have found many skeletons of these dinosaurs. *Protoceratops* was about the size of a pony. The adults were between 5 and 7 feet long. They weighed about 900 pounds.

The biggest dinosaur eggs ever discovered were found in southern France. These eggs were nearly round. They measured about 10 inches across. They were laid by a 35-foot dinosaur named *Hypselosaurus* (hip-sel-oh-SORE-us). Judging from its egg, a newly hatched *Hypselosaurus* weighed about 2 pounds. When it grew up, it weighed about 10 tons.

Hypselosaurus

Along with unhatched eggs, scientists have found the bones and skeletons of many baby dinosaurs. Some of these babies were amazingly small. The smallest one ever found was a baby *Psittacosaurus* (sit-uh-koh-SORE-us). It was barely 9 inches long. It could have crawled into a man's hands with plenty of room to spare. Its skull would fit easily on a fifty-cent piece.

Until recently, scientists thought that dinosaurs simply buried their eggs and left them. No baby dinosaur had ever been found in a nest. But in 1978, an important discovery was made by Robert Makela, a Montana high school teacher. He found a tangle of dinosaur bones about 75 million years old.

Makela studied the bones with the help of Dr. John Horner, a dinosaur expert from Princeton University. They belonged to fifteen baby *hadrosaurs* (had-ruh-SORZ), or duck-billed dinosaurs. Duckbills get their name from their broad, flat jaws, which looked something like a duck's bill.

The baby duckbills in Montana were huddled together in a mud nest near an ancient riverbank. Their nest was shaped like a bowl. It was about 7 feet across and 3 feet deep. The bottom of the nest was littered with broken eggshells.

The skull of a big dinosaur was found nearby. It was probably the babies' mother. No one knows what happened to kill all the dinosaurs at once.

The adult duckbill must have been about 35 feet long. The babies were about 3 feet long. Their teeth already showed signs of wear from chewing on coarse plants. They were at least a month or two old—but they were still living in their nest! Their mother was almost certainly taking care of them. If the babies had been on their own, they would have left their nest.

Other dinosaur nests were found close together in the same area. Some nests held unhatched eggs. Some held newly hatched babies about a foot-and-a-half long. And some held babies up to 5 feet long. They were several months old.

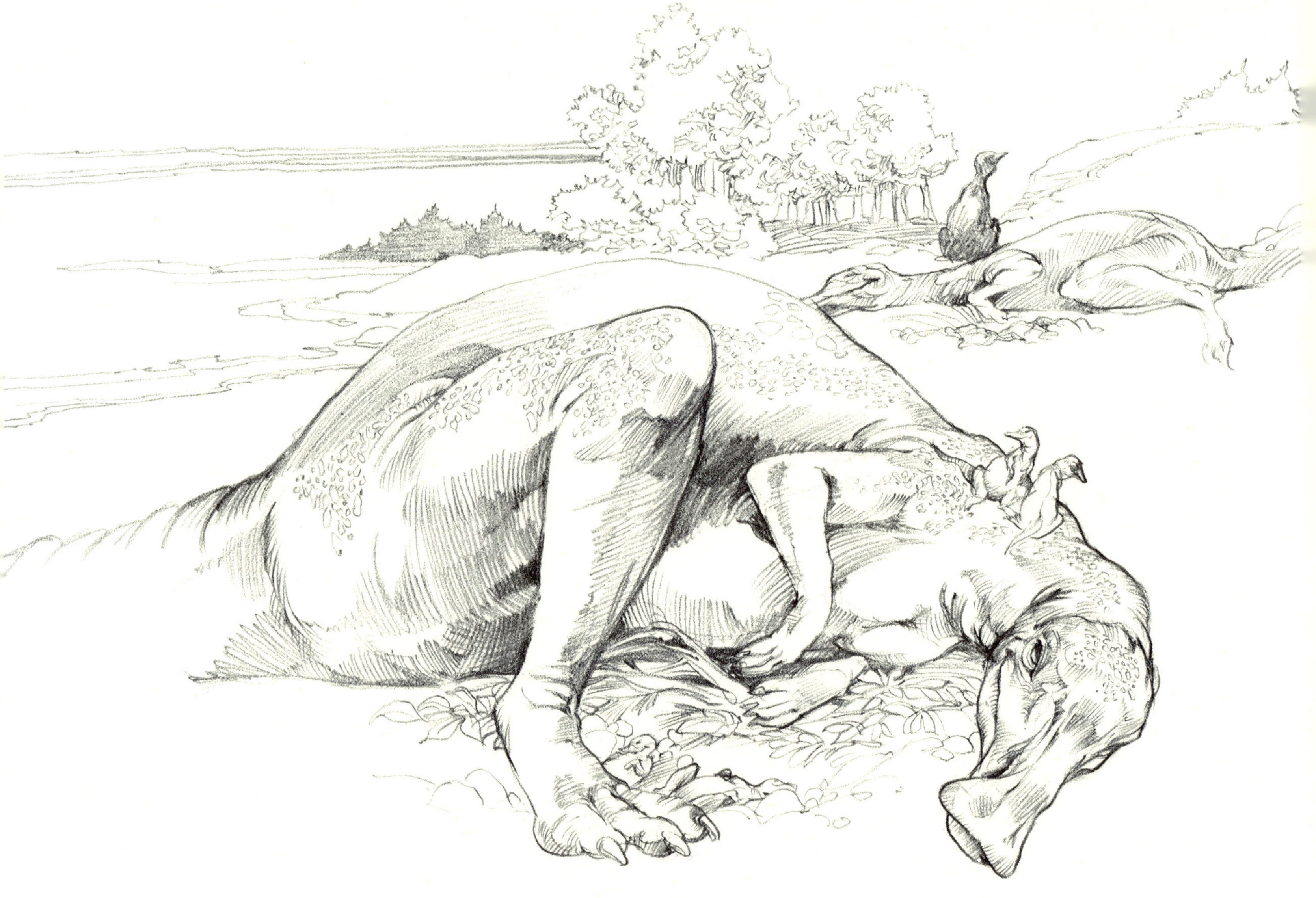

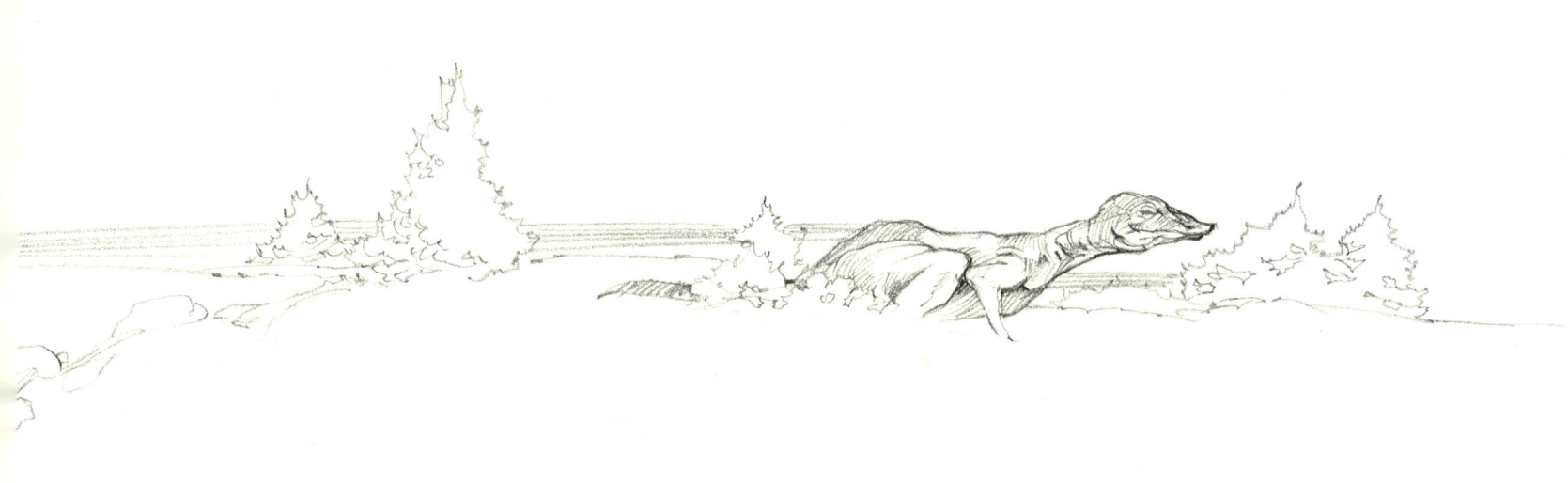

The nests near the river were a dinosaur nursery. Dr. Horner believes that duck-billed dinosaurs went there year after year to dig their nests, lay their eggs and raise their young.

Newly hatched duckbills may have been too weak to leave their nests. If so, their mothers had to bring food to them. They may have dragged boughs and saplings to the nest and heaped them in front of the little ones.

As the babies grew bigger, they were able to follow their mothers down to the river. Dr. Horner thinks that they fed in the river during the day and returned to their nests at night.

Far away from the nests, Dr. Horner found the bones of youngsters and adults who were probably feeding together. He guessed that when the young duckbills were old enough to feed themselves, they traveled with a herd of grown-ups. For protection, they may have traveled in the center of the herd.

All of the nests found in Montana belonged to duck-billed dinosaurs. But their bones show that they were a new kind of duckbill that had not been discovered before. Dr. Horner gave this new duckbill its name. He called it *Maiasaurus* (may-uh-SORE-us). The name means "good mother reptile."

At one time, duck-billed dinosaurs of many kinds were very common. Their bones have been found in Europe, Asia and North America. We know that full-grown duckbills were between 30 and 40 feet long—about as long as a city bus. They walked on their hind legs. When they stood upright they towered 10 to 20 feet above the ground.

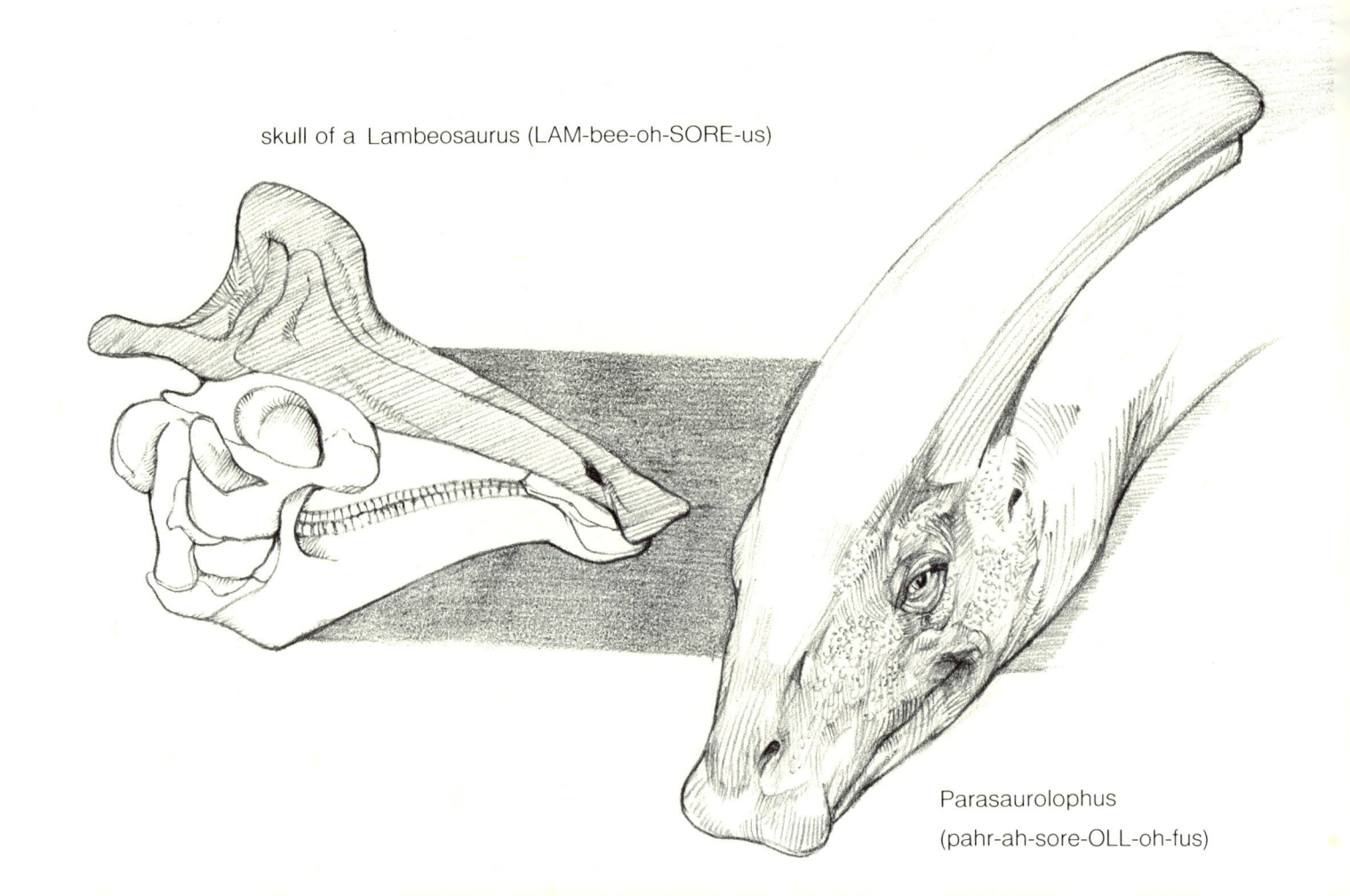

skull of a Lambeosaurus (LAM-bee-oh-SORE-us)

Parasaurolophus (pahr-ah-sore-OLL-oh-fus)

Saurolophus (sore-OLL-oh-fus)

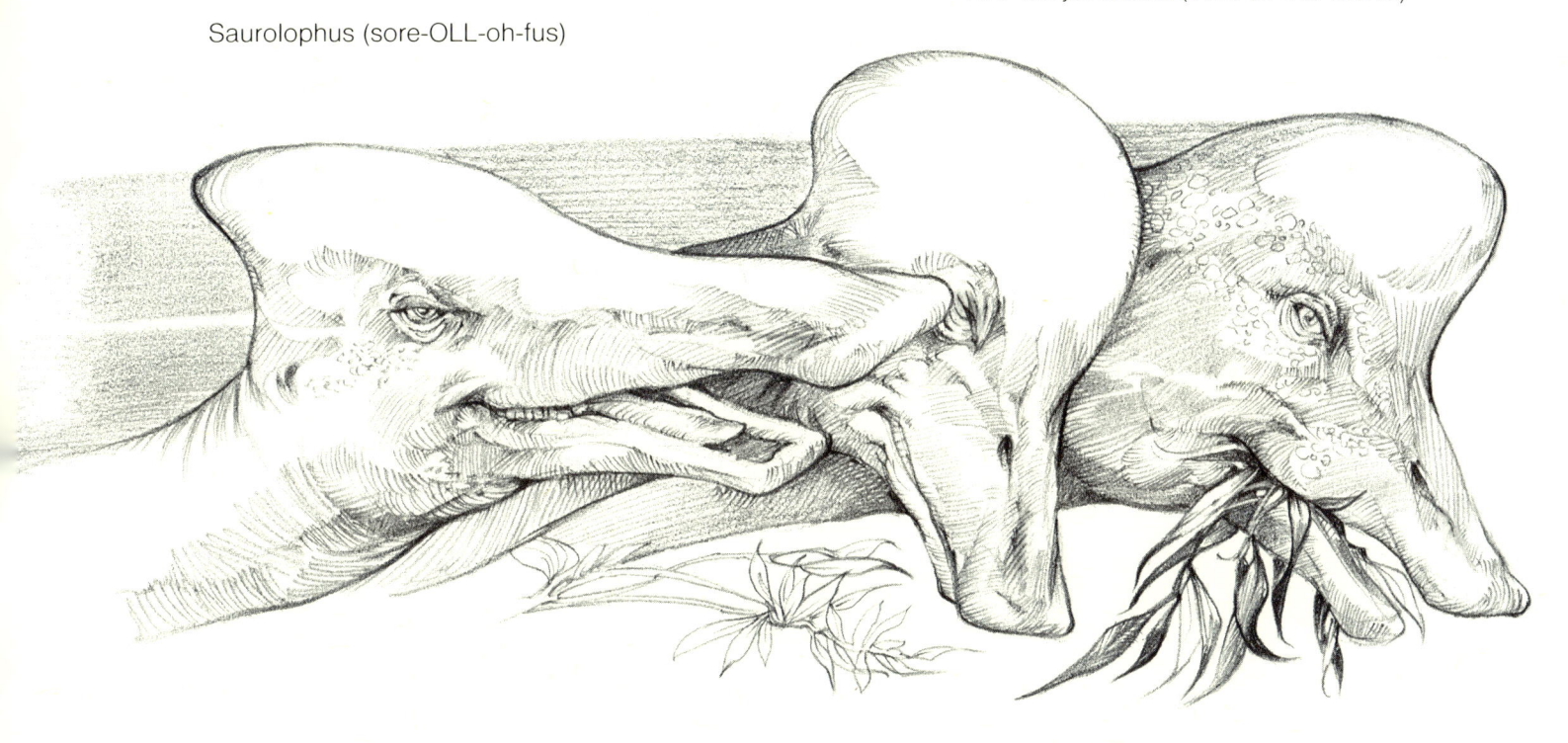

Two Corythosaurs (core-ee-tho-SORZ)

    Based on their discoveries, scientists have a good idea of how duckbills lived. They spent much of their time feeding in lakes, swamps and streams. They scooped up water plants with their duckbills, which were packed with hundreds of tiny teeth. The teeth worked like a huge grinder. Duckbills ground up coarse plants into a soft, mushy pulp that they could swallow easily. They must have eaten all the time to fill up their big bodies.

Some duckbills also went inland to find food in nearby forests. Standing upright, they ate needles from pine trees, leaves from magnolia trees, and seeds and fruits from many plants. Young duckbills must have stretched as high as they could reach for the tender buds and fresh new growth at the tops of trees.

Wherever they went, duckbills had to watch for enemies. Giant crocodiles lurked in the rivers and swamps. Fierce meat-eating dinosaurs hunted on land. The biggest and most terrible hunter was *Tyrannosaurus* (teh-ran-uh-SORE-us), which was nearly 50 feet long. Its huge jaws were armed with teeth lined up like daggers. Its open mouth looked like the entrance to a cave.

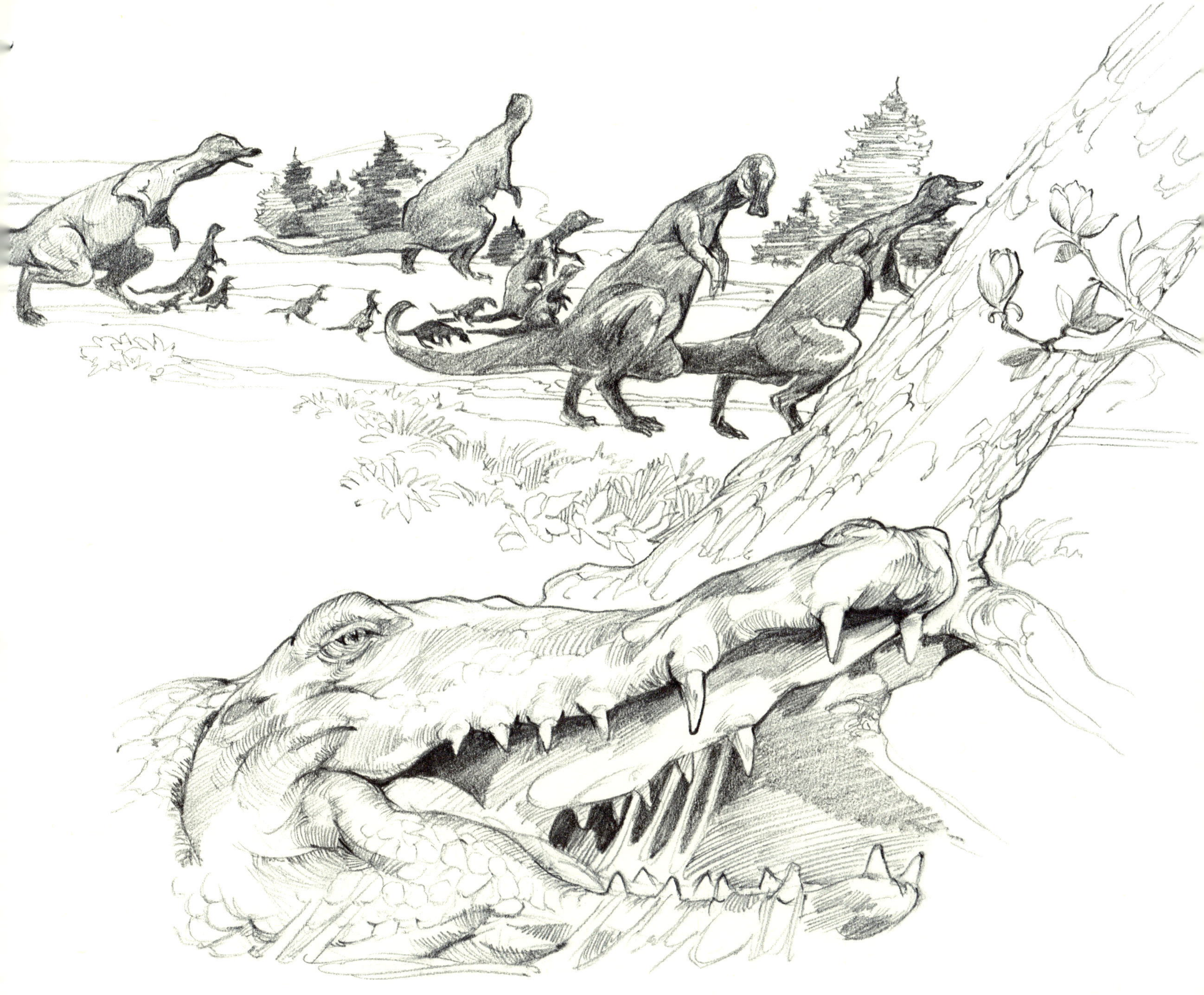

Tyrannosaurus

Full-grown duckbills were probably strong enough to fight off many of their enemies. They could bite hard with their beaks. And they could lash out with their powerful tails. But when big enemies like *Tyrannosaurus* came along, the duckbills had to run for their lives. They could probably run as fast as 30 miles an hour.

Duckbills seem to have had a keen sense of smell. When they smelled danger, they may have shrieked and bellowed as they raced for the nearest river or swamp. You can imagine them hurling themselves into the water with great splashes, swimming for safety. They were faster swimmers than most of their enemies.

Many young duckbills must have been caught and eaten by enemies. But many others escaped. They grew until they were big enough to fill their parents' footprints with footprints of their own.

If duck-billed dinosaurs cared for their young, it's possible that other dinosaurs did the same. Scientists now hope to find more nests, so they can learn more about the family life of dinosaurs.

31

INDEX

Asia, 24

Birds, 7

Crocodiles, 6, 9–10, 26

Duck-billed dinosaurs, 16, 18, 21–30

Eggs, 4, 6, 8, 10–15, 19, 21
Europe, 24

Fossils, 4
France, 13

Gobi desert, 10

hadrosaurs, *see* Duck-billed dinosaurs
Horner, Dr. John, 16, 21–22
Hypselosaurus, 13

Lizards, 6, 8, 10

Maiasaurus, 23
Makela, Robert, 15–16
Montana, 15–16, 23

North America, 24

Princeton University, 16
Protoceratops, 12
Psittacosaurus, 14

Reptiles, 6–7, 9

Snakes, 6, 8, 10

Turtles, 6, 8, 10
Tyrannosaurus, 26, 28